SIGNS
WONDERS
MIRACLES

Volume 2

ISBN: 978-1-990784-01-9

Published by Summit Global Publishing Ltd. on October 12, 2023

15203 75A St NW, Edmonton, AB
info@summitglobalpublishing.com

Compiled by Tracy Belford

Edited by Barbara Bearht, Tamar Smith, Tracy Belford

Cover by Krysta Koppel

Signs, Wonders, and Miracles:
Volume 2

Table of Contents

"So then faith comes by hearing, and hearing by the word of God." Romans 10:17 NKJV

Introduction

Have you ever wondered if God still works miracles? Or maybe if He only works miracles in far off places? Have you ever wondered if He would do a miracle for you?

This book has been compiled to answer those questions. It is a compilation of testimonies from all sorts of people who all happen to be connected to The Summit Church.

We aren't some special people or an extraordinary church; we are normal people. We are a church that believes the Bible is true and that Jesus said, *"These miraculous signs will accompany those who believe: They will cast out demons in my name, and they will speak in new languages. They will be able to handle snakes with safety, and if they drink anything poisonous, it won't hurt them. They will be able to place their hands on the sick, and they will be healed."* Mark 16:17-18 NLT

I pray as you read this, that you will be encouraged to ask Jesus for a miracle in your life, and that you will see Him do it in a way you never expected.

The greatest hindrance to miracles is a lack of faith. The paraplegic man that was let down on a mat through the roof was healed because of his friends' faith and their willingness to get him to a place in front of Jesus. Is it possible that God wants to increase your faith for your own miracle, or maybe even for someone else's?

I pray your faith for signs, wonders, and miracles would arise, and that through these testimonies, you would be changed and challenged to pray for miracles in your life, and the lives of those around you.

Tracy Belford

Heart Healing

While attending the True North conference at The Summit Edmonton Church, I started crying uncontrollably during worship. I heard the Lord say to me that I am beautiful. All of a sudden, every person in my life who had ever told me I was beautiful came flooding back to me: my husband, my aunts, my parents' friends, and people throughout my life. There were hundreds of people saying, "YOU ARE BEAUTIFUL".

The Lord was telling me that every time one of those people told me I was beautiful, it was actually Him telling me. The Lord had been telling me I was beautiful my whole life, but I never heard Him. I never listened, and I turned away from it.

You see, I was abused as a child when I was 5 years old and then again when I was 8. I never saw myself as beautiful. If anyone ever told me I was beautiful, I either thought they wanted something from me or they were lying. Also, I didn't want the extra attention put on me; I thought it would cause more pain and suffering.

These thoughts have shaped my being and caused me to not look people in the eye and be very introverted my whole life.

The Lord not only healed me of these feelings of unworthiness but showed me He has been there the whole time, loving me. Now when someone tells me I am beautiful, I welcome it and say, "Thank you." Knowing that the Lord sees my beauty is all I need. He is also telling me that I can help others see their beauty by telling them they are beautiful. One day the Lord will whisper to you and heal you of years of self-loathing too.

Kristy Kingsley, March 2022

I got an email from a lady who said that she had heard me testify about this woman, Brenda from Summit Cross City, who got healed of tumors from listening to my worship music. She took hold of that by faith. She said she played nothing but Summit Sounds worship albums for a whole month and that by the end of the month, she was completely set free from all of her anxiety and depression that she was experiencing. She attached her faith to someone else's testimony and got healed herself.

Nikki Mathis, February 2022

I spent the first year of my life in the hospital alone or in foster care. This left me with enormously deep-seated roots of abandonment, detachment, and a lack of self- worth. I was adopted just before my first birthday. My parents tried their best, but my mother had her own limitations, and she wasn't capable of being the kind of open-hearted mom I yearned for. This left me searching for a sense of belonging for most of my life. There was a time when I didn't respect or value my body or myself. I continuously made poor, impulsive decisions that took me farther from my true self. After being violated in my youth, further adding to my lack of self-worth, I landed in abusive relationships and eventually divorced from the father of my children.

I was raised in an atheist home that frowned upon God. I had experimented with different churches out of curiosity when I was young, but I had no true spiritual leaders in my life. I felt a sense of emptiness for most of my adult life.

When I met my current husband, we bonded over our disdain for religion. I didn't see us ever finding faith in God, the Almighty.

But then Covid happened and many of my beliefs in the world became fractured. As time went on, I found myself connecting with people who were Christ-focused, and I began questioning my past beliefs.

I expressed wanting to explore faith to my husband. And that's how we found The Summit. The True North Revival event in May 2022 randomly crossed my husband's Instagram feed. We thought we would come and check it out. That first night, I couldn't stop crying. I wanted, rather, I needed salvation, and I didn't know it. After the revival, I immediately wanted more. More Summit, more God, just more.

After that night, I couldn't get enough. I ran out and bought a baby Bible so I could read it really fast and get caught up on all of the 'stories' being shared during service. I have learned a lot! I bought a Bible small enough to fit in my purse so I could take it everywhere I went. My husband called me a woman on fire.

A week later, while I was exercising, I had a strong encounter with Jesus, and I declared Him as my Saviour. That was 8 months ago, and a lot has happened since then and I have had multiple examples of my prayers being answered.

I have a great story about getting a pretty incredible BBQ for my husband. That's when I first learned the power of praying out loud, and even of the little things God has beautifully crafted.

I also have a story about praying to God for random golf balls to appear—random because I don't play golf. My daughter and I were playing soccer and there was a golf ball in the middle of the field. At the time she and I were discussing if the Lord was real. So, I picked it up and told her we should pray to the Lord. Pray for random golf balls to show up to show us just how real He is. Throughout the next month, I randomly found 7 balls, in my work stuff, in our garage, and other places. It was 7 for a while, but I found another one about a month later. I believe it was God affirming a decision I had made. And now whenever I question my newfound beliefs, I think back to my bag of golf balls. A true and tangible sign the Lord is real.

Since becoming a believer, I was eager to get baptized. We had spoken to Pastor Chris Frost about it and found out November 6th would be the next Baptismal day.

But during the October True North Revival, on the Saturday night, there happened to be spontaneous baptisms. I couldn't believe it. Just that morning I had prayed to God "Please can I be baptized ASAP?" My prayer was answered that day and I got baptized. Hallelujah!

The next week was the Real and Raw Women's Conference where I had a huge breakthrough. Pastor Heather asked those around to lay their hands on me. After that day I've felt a huge transformational shift. I know I'm worthy. I know I'm a beloved daughter.

Psalm 139:13 TPT *"You formed my innermost being, shaping my delicate inside and my intricate outside, and wove them all together in my mother's womb."*

Ephesians 2:10 NLT *"For we are God's masterpiece. He has created us anew in Christ Jesus, so we can do the good things he planned for us long ago."*

I'm so excited to see what lies ahead now that I've laid my life before The Lord.

Shannon Westervelt, November 2022

I grew up in a Christian home, so I learned about Jesus at a very young age. When I was about 5, I asked Jesus into my heart, alone, in my bedroom. I remember that day vividly and the overwhelming joy that followed my prayer of surrender and running to tell my mom. From that day on I was a sponge for all things Jesus. I was consumed with spreading the gospel and pleasing the Lord.

When I was about 11, the devil crept in through the door of anxiety, panic attacks, and stage fright. Before this, I had won awards each year for public speaking at my elementary school, and after this, I was crippled with fear. For 27 years, I was a slave to my flesh and worldly pleasures, getting stuck in a deep addiction to alcohol. In June 2022, I had had enough, and I knew I had to give my life to God again.

After I was reborn, Jesus did not hesitate to open my spiritual eyes. My life was changed. The Lord then slowly started leading me to people and places that helped me in my walk with Him and one of those places was Deliverance/Revival Ministry. When I saw what the Lord was doing in His children through the gifts of the Holy Spirit, I was in awe. That's when the Lord led me to Google late one night. I Googled "Revival Churches Edmonton" and found The Summit Edmonton Church, and even better, I saw that their True North Revival service was coming up that weekend. I was so thankful to God!

I attended with my mom on Saturday, September 3rd. I went with the expectation of experiencing God's perfect love. All I wanted was to glorify Him. Well, the Lord did not disappoint. I could feel His presence the minute I walked in. After finding a seat, I decided to make a commitment to God that He could show up in me in whatever way He wanted and that I wouldn't allow my perception of the way others may see me stop me from being in the Spirit. It was near the end of worship when I could physically feel the Holy Spirit. Without warning, my body began to shake, I started to cry tears of joy, uncontrollable tears, and out of my mouth a shriek "Jesus! Jesus!" That's all I could manage to yell, but it was exactly what was on my heart. It came from deep in my belly and I could feel heat accumulating. Not painful, just very noticeable. My teeth were even chattering.

It was an incredible feeling of release. Freedom. Jesus was here and He was here for me. The rest of the night felt a bit like a blur, but I remember Pastor Chris Mathis prophesying over me after his sermon, telling me that the Lord was saying He's proud of me; He's proud to call me His daughter and He sees me, and it's ok to be seen by the Father. Wow! Jesus came, and He came for me. At the end of the evening, Chris had asked anyone who needed freedom from addiction to come to the front, so I did. At the time, I truly thought I was all out of tears, but the Lord had other plans. I knelt in front of the stage and immediately was swept up into Jesus' presence. Once again, tears of joy flowed. It was in that moment I felt a hand on my lower back and one on my heart from one of the ministry team leaders and though I couldn't hear what they were praying over me, I could feel them tap my lower back where I had been experiencing a lot of pain. As their hand moved up my back, I could feel the pain, like a burning ember, move up until it was in my throat and then released. I stood up after that and felt such a deep peace and joy. What a night! Thank you to the entire Summit Church ministry team. I'm so grateful God led me to you. Hallelujah! Thank you, Jesus.

Cynthia Meinke, September 2022

Answered Prayers

One day in January, after the church service, a lady came up to me. She'd waited for a while because I was talking to other people. When I finally got a chance to talk to her, she had tears in her eyes. She said, "Pastor, this is my first time at Summit. The last point you preached was that prayers that you've been praying for years are going to start finding you. I was divorced five years ago, and I haven't talked to any of my kids in five years. They've been very bitter and upset. At the end of the message you gave, I went to the foyer to go out and give something in the offering. And when I came back in, I had a tap on my shoulder. I turned around and it was my son! It was also his first Sunday at Summit. We are going to lunch together and we're going to sit down and talk."

Summit Pastoral Staff, January 2022

My daughter's teacher has had an altar to the dead set up in the classroom (a supposed Christian program). My daughter, Alina, was really upset when one week after my grandma passed away, her teacher asked if she could put a picture of my grandma on that altar as other kids had done.

I didn't know about the altar until Alina came home upset. I went and saw it for myself. It was complete with skulls, candles, and ribbons, and it was really creepy. When I asked the School Logos board representative, I was told that they had tried to get the principal to take it down but were having no luck.

I wanted to email the school right away, but I got distracted. At 1:30 a.m., I woke up suddenly and heard God say, "Don't email until you intercede for the principal."

I was tired, barely awake, and remember saying to God, "No, not for her. I don't like her at all. And I'm tired, and I need to get to work super early today."

But I did it. Sort of. I'm somewhat ashamed to say that it was very half-hearted, and there may have been an internal eye roll with it. I was just not there in my heart.

I sent an email around noon, and within an hour, the principal emailed me back and said she would have the teacher remove the altar. Praise God. Furthermore, she took my suggestion that the students have a prayer wall instead, a place where they could post requests and share how God answered. She is completely against anything Christian, so I was shocked! No fight, nothing.

And next time, I'll be a little less resistant. But God was still so good despite my less than genuine heart.

Beki Ryzuk, November 2022

My car has been in rough shape since I got it in 2020. It's a 2007 and it seems like it hit a wall mechanically; everything on it went.

I was driving from Calgary to Edmonton in February and my tire blew out. I came home for Reading Week, needing a new car before the end of the week because I knew that I couldn't make it back to Calgary with it.

On Sunday, I gave an offering believing God for a car. Thursday came, which was cutting it a little close. I gave some more money believing it was in God's hands.

That night, I received a gift from someone who heard about my car troubles and wanted to help. I had a family friend who was a mechanic. On Saturday, he offered me a good deal on a car he had, and I was able to buy the car from him. I was able to drive home from Calgary the next day and the car has been great for six months!

Brett Meeberg, March 2023

Testimonies About Moving

This family will go where God calls us!

Those are the closing lines of what we wrote in 2016 as our family statement. When you write those words, you imagine that God will tell you to go and move to the next block or maybe to make some changes in your daily life. We never thought those words would mean moving to another country one day. For some families, Covid was a stage that they disliked. For us, it meant so many good things. We were no longer running late every morning in a big traffic jam taking our daughters to school. We felt peace inside our home in the middle of many questions and many oppressions. That steadiness set us apart from our many ministerial activities and brought our family closer to what God had for us.

We started making plans and focusing on our future; one project was buying land to build our house in our beautiful country, Guatemala. I remember we took a picture of the entrance to this land and thought: *is this what God wants for us?* That day, an old friend from school wrote to me and showed me a picture of a similar place. The difference was that the place was in Canada. My heart jumped and it was like my eyes were opened. Suddenly, I turned to my husband and asked him, "Would you move to Canada?" His immediate answer was "Yes!"

For days we prayed, and I also spent days researching and daydreaming. The most critical questions I had for God were when and where. When something is in my mind, I get very intense in asking the same question repeatedly. It doesn't matter what I am doing. Whenever we don't hear God's voice, we don't decide.

Over the next few days, three special events happened. First, a friend sent me a YouTube video of how God was moving people to other countries. I watched the video and took notes because it was so good. Second, I was doing chores at home and repeating the same questions until I heard loud and clear, "Alberta". I stopped and just waited. It was so clear that I got excited. That same day, a friend from our church prayed for us. I remember talking to her on the phone and feeling my heart beating so fast. We scheduled a video call, and while conversing regularly, she stopped and said some letters. She clearly said the letters didn't mean anything to her, that she did not understand, and spelled E, D, M, O, N, T, and repeated, "Edmonton?"

Then there was the paperwork. We were still in the middle of Covid, and many people thought we were crazy. We had to renew our passports, and the waiting time was six to eight months, but we made it in less than a month. God provided everything. In a sea of *don't have*, He made it all possible. At every step of the way, He gave us a word that kept us standing. We were confident that this idea started in God's heart for our family.

We searched Google for churches in Edmonton, and that is how we found The Summit. We knew it would take a while for us to be there. God gave us the next instruction: "*Not by sight, by faith.*" That is how we started watching the online services for one year. Sometimes it was frustrating when people from our other church asked why we had stopped congregating since we still were in Guatemala. But we knew God had a plan. As much as we wanted to think that we moved for better opportunities for our family, in our hearts, we always knew there was more.

When we arrived in Edmonton, many things happened; good and bad, but there was always good in the bad. God came through at the last moment for housing, college, and more.

Our daughters got sick many times for months because of the many changes; even on the first day we arrived, they started feeling sick. Being away from Guatemala was difficult. We did not know anyone in Edmonton. The next day, we arrived and went to The Summit. Even though we were going through so many changes for several months, we looked forward to going to church on Sunday.

As we were missing our family and going through financial difficulties, I remember one day I said to God that I felt out of place. I had that crazy idea of not belonging anywhere and being so sad that day we went to church. In the middle of the service, someone approached us and prayed. That was the faith we needed at that moment. The word *home* came to us over and over, many times, until one day Pastor Chris preached and spoke about the importance of starting to call this land HOME. We understood that we were referring to Guatemala as home the whole time, and we needed to marry the land to which God brought us.

A year has passed, and tears of joy come every time I remember many stories of God's actions. But the most important thing is that He has worked in our hearts for a year. Two years ago, I sang a song every day, "All I Want," by Pastor Nikki. I know that is precisely what God has done. He has been taking every layer of religion, and He has renewed our minds. We have met Him differently, and if that was the purpose of Him bringing us to Edmonton, it has all been worth it.

Jocelyn Gonzalez, March 2023

I'm a teacher. I moved in faith from Fort McMurray, leaving a permanent contract. I asked God to please give me a job by the time I get my last paycheck from my other school board.

Competition is very tough here for teachers. But today, I got a job at Covenant Christian School in Leduc (Black Gold School Division). It is part-time, but I can sub when not working!

I start tomorrow. And my last paycheck from Fort McMurray Public is tonight at midnight. God is awesome.

Anonymous, August 2022

Physical Healings

We had ordered new chairs for our West Summit location. The delivery driver was a Muslim. He came from a Muslim family here in Canada and had some Christian family in India that were really hurt by scam Christianity, so he had suspicions about Christianity. He was telling me why he doesn't believe while I prayed for him. Then he noticed healing happening in his foot. Later, he came to a church service and brought his wife. I got an Instagram from him, and he said his brother had the same problem with his foot. So, we prayed for his brother. Then his brother Instagramed me and said, "Hey, I want prayer because my foot is in so much pain." So, the brother came to church. A few people started praying for him. He had never had people lay hands on him before; he came from a completely different culture. He was so humble. After being prayed for, he said, "What's going on here?" He got totally healed. He said, "The pain is all gone." He could do stuff with his foot that he usually couldn't.

TJ Green, February 2022

A lady from church messaged me saying she wanted to get the message that was preached last Sunday at the East location. She said she was healed from strep throat while listening online and needed to listen to it again.

Anonymous, February 2022

My husband and I travelled to Zambia in November. He is the International Missions Director for an organization in Zambia and was holding several conferences for their pastors. This meant lots of sitting during the flights, sitting during the conference (with non-stop bugs flying through my hair), and sitting while travelling to the different locations, so I did not get as much movement over the 3 weeks as I normally would. When I got home, I had terrible pain in my hip flexors and pelvic area on both legs. I had regular physio appointments to try to lengthen the muscles that tightened. It was painful to walk, sleep, etc., as most movement involved my hips.

During the service one Sunday morning, one of the girls got up and spoke about how God wants to heal muscles in the exact areas where I was having terrible pain. She mentioned the exact symptoms I had been experiencing and she said specifically on the right side. My right side had been more painful than the left. When she prayed, the pain immediately left my right side and has not returned.

My miracle! I could feel the muscles on the left side lengthening and relaxing as she was praying. After the service, the pain on my left side was 50% better. I decided to go to the gym in the afternoon and run as long as I could so that I could test my body.

Normally, this would have resulted in debilitating pain, especially the next morning. I was so excited to go to sleep and wake up to test out my left side. The next day there was very little pain on my left side, and it was 75% better. My husband and I kept claiming healing over my body and today the pain is completely gone. So grateful God is my healer and that I attended church on Sunday.

Paula Bonk, January 2023

One Sunday, a child had a cracked kneecap, and his pain was at a level 7. I had prayed for him during worship, and he said, "I can't breathe, something is pushing on my lungs." I prayed over that and then it lifted.

In Kid's Church, the same child asked for prayer. I asked who had faith to see him healed, and 3 kids raised their hands. They prayed. We gently held out his legs and the kids commented how the hurt one was 1-2 inches shorter than the other. I got them all to watch, and as I prayed, his leg became the same length as the other.

All the kids freaked out. I asked, "Now who has faith to see him healed?" This time the whole room raised their hands and started to pray. That's when the pain dropped down to a 5. He was able to straighten his leg with no additional pain, but bearing weight still hurt.

One girl had a headache that was instantly healed. One girl had overextended her finger, and it felt immediately better. One boy came in with a sore foot and it stopped hurting. God is working miracles in Kid's Church!

Beki Ryzuk, May 2022

I had been fit-tested for an N95 mask at my work and it was there that the nurse had told me that I had a deviated septum in my nose, and it stripped me of my sense of taste and smell.

At the May 7th True North Revival service, Pastor TJ had a word that someone in the church had lost their sense of taste and smell due to a deviated septum and that the Lord wanted to heal it that night.

My plan was to schedule an appointment to get surgery done, but it looks as though I won't be needing to anymore, because I have been touched and healed. Thank you, Jesus, that You love me so much to perform and demonstrate such a miraculous act to make it known that you surely see me.

Andrew Harnum, June 2022

I was born with a neurological congenital progressive disease that started at conception, and it was relentless. There is no effective medical treatment or cure for this disease. I could walk without too much trouble as a kid, but I was always the kid with scraped knees and sprained ankles. I constantly dropped things. I underwent several foot surgeries to stabilize my feet, but they were not successful. As I aged, the disease progressed. Depending on the circum-stance, for the last 25 years I have used a walker, a cane, or a power chair whenever I left my home. My hands also became extremely weak.

On April 17, 2022, God began the process of healing my body during an online prayer meeting over Zoom, part of the online ministry school I recently graduated from. The person leading the meeting asked us to stand if we had a need or if we were interceding for someone else. I didn't stand for myself that day. I stood for three people in my online ministry school who are wheelchair users.

As I stood, I realised my legs weren't hurting. Usually, my quad muscles would burn after standing unaided for only 20 seconds. I was standing for one minute and then two. By that time, people could see something happening and were asking questions. I was trying to type as I stood, leaning over my desk. By the time everyone calmed down, it was 5 minutes. I then pointed out that I was only wearing house slippers, not my leg braces.

Less than a week after this encounter, I could walk and move for over an hour at a time, with no pain and with no stumbling. I was using my walker as a glorified purse carrier more than anything else. Severe neuropathy receded. The deadening of nerves caused this neuropathy, which resulted in muscle loss and foot and hand deformities. For the first time in as long as I can remember, my feet began to sweat as they should when they are overheated. My nerves were being resurrected from the dead.

On April 30, 2022, my 65th birthday, I received prayer in person while in Redding, California. God was not done! I have lived with a severe speech impediment for most of my life. It is now 90% improved, and it continues to improve daily. God also restored my deltoid muscles in both arms. My hands are a work in progress, but I am now able to use tongs! No longer do I have to avoid buffets because now I can serve myself!

Two weeks before my healing began, my eye doctor mentioned that I might need a second surgery on one eyelid. It appeared to him that the surgery I underwent several years prior was failing. After receiving prayer, that eyelid lifted on its own.

I give God glory for everything He has done for me and continues to do. More healing is needed, but as I give thanks for every improvement, no matter how slight, I see more improvement. If you or a loved one have lived with a chronic illness or disability for decades, take hope from my testimony. I am proof God heals today. I did nothing special. I didn't have to pray fancy words. I didn't have to take a course on how to be healed. I didn't need a famous healing evangelist to pray for me. I didn't need to repent. I didn't have to forgive anyone or ask forgiveness for anything. I just needed to receive it.

Perhaps someone has told you that God allowed you to suffer from your illness for His glory. Let me counteract that thought. If a parent places their child's hand on a hot stove to prove a point, that parent would be arrested for child abuse. Our heavenly Father is a good Father and never causes His children to suffer to teach them a lesson or to prove a point. Healing testifies of God's glory much more than suffering ever could. My prayer for you is quite simple. Be healed in Jesus' name.

Katherine Walden, May 2022

One Sunday, a woman walked through the door for the 11:30 a.m. service. Once I had greeted her, she looked surprised and responded, "I can smell!" I asked her what she meant. She went on to explain that she had lost her sense of smell back in 2020 due to Covid. She said when she came in, she could smell for the first time since 2020.

She was so excited, and so was I! God is good. I didn't even pray for her. I just welcomed her, and as she walked through the door, God restored her smell!

Rachel Rintala, March 2023

One Saturday night, my son, Elijah, slipped and fell. He banged his head and didn't tell me for hours. Eventually, he showed me and told me how much his head was killing him, and that he was dizzy. I realized he probably had a concussion.

I told him I would pray for him, but he just wanted to leave the church service. Then Pastor Jamie prayed for him. He texted me a while later during worship and said that his head was hurting a lot more, especially because it was so loud. He wanted to go home and rest.

After about 20 minutes of worship, Jesus spoke to him and said that he should not leave. Then he was spontaneously healed.

Tracy Belford, April 2022

The year began with a 22 day fast. My time with the Lord was deeper than it had ever been before. Prayer time on the Battle For Canada Wall was precious and connected in great love and power.

On March 7, during an oil fast, God told me He was going to give me a new heart. I remember being so elated. At that time, I believed He meant that he was going to change my heart of stone to a soft heart.

On April 17, I tested positive for Covid. The following day, I had a near death experience. At that time, I remember God clearly telling me that He will never leave me; I am set apart and precious in His sight. Even though I could not move my body, I had a great sense of peace and love. I saw a bright light and felt the presence of my mother and aunt Blanche. I could not see them, but I was positive it was them. Love and protection surrounded me. I was so cocooned. I remained for a time.

After this I began having greater issues with my breathing and angina. This was the point that I realised that God was talking about my actual beating heart. I asked my sister, Sandy, to take me to the emergency department in Lacombe. The doctor referred me to a heart specialist.

The referral came through at the office where Sandy worked, so she rushed the order, and my tests were done on May 5th and 6th. In the late afternoon of the 6th, I asked Sandy to take me back to Lacombe Hospital. I was then admitted and told I would be transported to Edmonton.

My appointment was set for May 9 at 2:00 p.m.; We arrived by ambulance just before noon, and I was immediately rolled into the Cath lab. After the exam, I was told I would be transferred to Mazankowski for open heart surgery.

The surgery was set for the morning of the 13th. An emergency came in the early hours of the morning, so it got pushed back to the afternoon.

My son, Logan, walked with me to the doors of the operating theatre. Prayers were sent to heaven and there was great peace in the atmosphere. I never doubted for a moment that God's hands were all over this event in my life.

The next thing I remember was seeing Logan and talking about the success of the surgery. On the 20th, I was released from the hospital into the care of my good nursing friend, Rhona. Her son, David, much to my surprise, was very protective and served my every need. On June 12, I arrived back home in Lacombe County.

On August 17, I was scheduled for my first shift at work even when I felt that I was not ready. I asked my sister to get me an appointment with a new heart doctor, Dr. Tilley, who called me that night and we did blood tests the following day. Dr. Tilley told me I would be going back to Edmonton for another procedure.

The procedure was booked for August 31. It showed my heart was in the worst condition, with two 100% blockages and two 90% blockages. Imagine the protective hand of God, who protected me while I drove myself to Edmonton.

No one could have guessed the vein in the back of my heart had collapsed. That day, a very skilled doctor did a very complex reconstruction on my heart. My blood pressure is now better than when I was 20 years old. All praise and glory go to God, our Father.

Brenda White, August 2022

I was in a car accident about 12 years ago, and I injured my right knee very badly. And so, I've seen multiple knee surgeons, had MRIs, tests, all you can think of. They told me that as I get older, I would have multiple reconstructive knee surgeries, have an arthritic knee, and be in pain for the rest of my life. But I can tell you now, I have not had any pain since January when Jesus healed me!

Anonymous, September 2022

I had a migraine last night from around dinner time till about 9pm. I took six or seven Acetaminophen with codeine and two Advil. A friend tried to help with a back massage, a cold cloth, and a dark room. Nothing worked.

My head pounded and pounded. It was awful. If you've had a migraine, then you totally get what I mean with this. At one point, with tears running down my face, I said, "Father, everyone says if I need You to just ask, so I'm asking You to take the pain. I'm laying it before You. I don't want it; take away this headache, in Jesus' name!"

Within 15 minutes or so, it was gone!

Anonymous, June 2023

Miracles of Birth

Labour began at 12:30 a.m. while everyone else was sleeping. My husband, Shane, woke up at 2:00 a.m. with a sick child, Skyler. I then told him that I was in labour and contracting every 3 minutes. Thankfully, Papa and Nana came quickly! By the time we got to Grey Nuns Hospital, I went from 3 to 8 cm in a short two hours. Maverick was born at 6:15 a.m. at 5 pounds 9 ounces. The doctors said he was only 37 weeks in the womb, not 40 as we had thought. The cord was knotted! If your baby's umbilical cord gets a knot early on, the baby's growth and future movements can tighten the knot, squeezing off blood and oxygen to the baby.

Maverick couldn't breathe upon delivery and was rushed to NICU with an amazing team. I immediately prayed and reached out to our pastors and friends, begging them to pray for Maverick. I was left in labour and delivery knowing nothing about what was going on. He had help breathing with oxygen and breathing suction. Two hours later, I went to the NICU to see him, and they offered to take him off and let him be breastfed. You could imagine Shane's and my fear of this. However, Maverick immediately began to feed and did NOT need oxygen again. He was released with me to postpartum care and has not showed one sign of any struggle. The nurse that came on shift when he was taken off oxygen was in complete shock that he ever had any issues. Miracles happen daily, people! God showed me a miracle today and gave me another perfect son to care for and love. Isaiah 66:13 says, *"As one whom his mother comforts, so I will comfort you."* Thank you, God, our friends, our church, and the staff here at Grey Nuns Hospital.

Cheryl Lamothe, January 2023

In September 2021, my wife, Denai, found out she was pregnant. At 8 weeks, we went to get an ultrasound to see our baby. But when we went in, the radiologist told us that we didn't have a baby. Instead, it was a molar pregnancy, which we had never heard of before. It essentially fools your body into acting as if it were pregnant and starts growing a tumour instead.

Upon hearing this news, we wanted to get a second opinion from an OBGYN because we read that there were a lot of cases wherein the molar pregnancy was misdiagnosed and they later found out that it was a viable fetus. We were believing for a fetus.

We went to the OBGYN, and they confirmed that they believed it to be a molar pregnancy. They advised Denai to get a D&C as soon as possible as there was the possibility of it developing complications that could threaten future pregnancies, or even develop into cancer. Disappointed by this news, we still wanted to wait a while longer to see if God would give us a creative miracle of molar pregnancy to real pregnancy, and to negate any chance of aborting a viable fetus.

After waiting a few weeks, Denai started to experience red flag symptoms, and so, we went to the OBGYN to get one final look at an ultrasound to look for a fetus. He confirmed it to still be a molar pregnancy. Devastated, we agreed to schedule the D&C the next day. The D&C was completed on October 26, 2021. Following the procedure, Denai had to go in for blood work once a week to ensure the HCG levels decreased. If they did not decrease, she was informed that she may need chemo-therapy.

For us, the worst part about the D&C wasn't just that it was the final nail in our hopes for a miraculous pregnancy, but also the fact that our OBGYN advised us to not try to get pregnant again for one year following the D&C because of the increased chance of complications that might arise from parts of the molar cell remaining in the uterus or possible recurring molar pregnancies. We were also told that after the D&C, it was not likely that Denai would be able to get pregnant very easily. We were excited to have a baby nine months from September 2021, so to have to wait another 21 months was devastating.

Upon bringing our devastation to the Lord, we both felt complete peace that once Denai's cycle came back that we would go against the doctor's orders and begin trying for a baby right away.

41

The week that we began trying was also the week of Denai's birthday. Denai had asked God for a birthday gift in hopes that He would graciously gift us with a child. On January 7th, 2022, which was also the day of her birthday, we were at the True North Revival Conference where they asked for those looking for a miracle in their body to come to the altar. Denai felt in her spirit she was to go to the altar.

Pastor Chris laid hands and prayed over Denai. He said "Lord, thank You for the child that You are sending to Denai." But then he stopped and corrected himself saying, "No. I thank You for the child that is with Denai right now."

Two weeks later, Denai took a pregnancy test, and it was positive! Looking back at the timing of her cycle, we realized the night Pastor Chris declared the bold prayer that our child was with Denai, it was true! Our precious baby was being knit together in Denai's womb the night that this prayer was prayed. On September 23, 2022, our beautiful healthy baby boy, Selah Israel Wiebe, was born. We give all the glory to God for this miracle!

Christian Wiebe, September 2022

I had asked for prayer on May 20, 2023, over my irregular periods. I went to my doctor on June 6th, and he told me that I hadn't had a period in a very long time and all my periods were missed, which essentially meant that I was not ovulating. So, he sent me for PCOS and hormone testing. All of my tests came back normal.

That night my husband and I declared healing over my body, and for the first time in all my life, I started a normal period on June 7th.

We went to The Summit on June 14th, and my husband went up for prayer. During a prophetic word, Joel asked him if he was a father. My husband said no, and Joel told him he would be a spiritual father of many and a father of his own. Then on June 18th, before I went to sleep, the Lord showed me the name Solomon.

Later that week, I asked God to show my husband a vision of our child to confirm our pregnancy, and on June 25th, while in worship, my husband saw a vision of our son (I had never told him about my prayer!)

We also had two friends who told us that they had a word or vision from God telling them I was pregnant.

After my blood work today, it is confirmed I am in fact pregnant!

Anonymous, July 2023

Deliverance

I was struggling with extreme exhaustion and shortness of breath shortly after Christmas. I had also been hit with heavy depression during the beginning of January that was also accompanied by thoughts of suicide. The emotional pain combined with the tiredness and difficulties in breathing were too much for me some days and it got very dark to the point where I just wanted it all to end. This had not been the first time that I struggled with these exact symptoms; I had also been sick for most of 2020.

I had been in touch with my intercessory group about the physical limitations I was having, and they had been praying for me. As a part of the intercessory group, I was supposed to be at church early for prayer before the True North service on February 4 and 5, but because of my struggles, my leader suggested that I stay home on Friday. So, I was at home livestreaming the service when Ron Teal started preaching about how it's easy to get someone healed, but it's hard to keep them that way. He then referred to people holding their reoccurring symptoms close like a little baby. That convicted me so strongly. It was like an arrow to my heart. Right then, I knew that was what I had been doing.

I finished watching the service, and at the end, as Ron was praying for everyone, I got down on my face in my living room. As I was praying, I heard Pastor Nikki start talking about how people felt like they were in a dark room and immediately I knew that was me. She said to go down the hallway even if you needed to feel along the wall and go open the windows and the doors.

I lost track of what she was saying after that because I was so overtaken by what I was going through. I knew that I had chosen to stay in that dark room and hadn't even thought to open a window. I felt the Holy Spirit come in and start to do many things in my heart. I began repenting of things and I felt suicide and depression break off of me.

Then God reminded me of what Ron Teal had just been talking about regarding illness and I felt the Holy Spirit convict me that I had been using illness to protect myself from a very young age. He showed me that I had chosen to partner with illnesses of all sorts over the years and used them as a way of keeping people away, as a way of controlling the amount of "things" life threw at me and to generally protect myself from life. I repented of all of it and for letting these things get in the way of my relationship with the Father. I saw how my self-protection actually put a barrier between Him and me.

Then, I went through a time of repenting of whatever the Holy Spirit brought to my mind. At one point, I was sitting on the floor, and I saw a big blue snake being twisted and pulled out of my body. As I laid on the floor again, I felt His forgiveness like a stream of fresh water wash over me, washing everything away, and then, I felt Jesus come into me. After a long while on the floor, I got up and sat down on the couch. I realized that I was not tired anymore. This was very strange given what I had just been through and that it was late in the evening. But I felt rejuvenated and no longer had the symptoms that I had been struggling with for almost two months. No more breathing problems and no more exhaustion! I had a very busy weekend after this experience and the symptoms did not return. I write this a week since these events and the symptoms have not returned. But as Ron Teal said, I am being diligent to not accept them back.

Jennifer Trudeau, January 2022

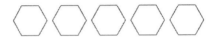

I didn't want to go. I grabbed my car keys and stood at the door. I was all dressed for the winter weather with my feet glued to the floor and my eyes glued to the door. I was having an argument with myself. I knew that I should go because the night before Pastor TJ spoke on how God responds to my response. "Don't ask God to do something that I myself should do!" he spoke. So, I kicked myself in the butt, opened the door, locked it, and dragged my bad attitude to the garage to go to church. I felt nothing!

At church, I spoke to a couple and told them how much of a struggle it was to get there that night. The man told me that he had been dealing with high anxiety and fear too. Then he prophesied that God would touch both of us that night to which I heartily agreed by faith. I still felt nothing.

Worship began and, as usual, it was heartfelt and powerful. Many times, Pastor Nikki said that you didn't have to feel anything. You just know that God is worthy and worship Him. So, that is what I did. I clapped my hands, danced, and sang loudly because the King was worthy. My beautiful friend, Jen, came over and gave me a huge hug. I felt so loved. I worshiped some more and then heard something in my head: "I want you to confess feeling suicidal to Wendy." (Wendy was on my left.) I thought, "NO WAY!" That can't be God. We sang some more and then I leaned over to Jen on my right. I said, "Jen, I just want to confess something to you. I want to confess feeling suicidal." She immediately grabbed me and told me how blessed she was the night before and how God had wrecked her in her living room watching the livestream. She was battling some stuff and God had set her free. She proceeded to pray for me. I still felt nothing.

Worship was wrapping up and Pastor Chris mentioned a young man wanted to commit suicide the night before. He was attending again tonight. The young man expressed his pain and anguish, and that he felt he couldn't even commit suicide right. I felt his pain. He said that God had told him to go to The Summit and he got set free. Pastor Chris then said that he felt there were others attending that night that needed the same freedom. He asked those who were afflicted with this evil to raise their hands and receive prayer. I looked at Jen and asked if I should put my hand up. I mean, Jen had dealt with that, right? I already covered that. But no, Jen gave me "the look" and told me with her eyes what to do. So, I raised my hand and still felt nothing.

Immediately, I was surrounded by love. Wendy, the lady who I was first supposed to confess to, started to pray for me. I hate making a scene. I don't manifest. But as Wendy started to pray, I felt contractions in my mid-section. That caused me to bend forward. I didn't like that I wasn't put together, so I immediately forced myself straight up. Then it happened again. I bent down, and again felt something like labor contractions in my mid-section. Wendy commanded me to stay bent down. My treacherous body obeyed her. I don't remember what she prayed next, but I then found myself screaming. I don't scream. I don't scream. The person who doesn't scream was screaming like a banshee. I was livid. I felt all the pent-up fear, anxiety, ANGER, and suicide leave me with each scream. I thought I could scream forever in that moment. It felt good. But then Wendy said, "That's enough!" And once again, my treacherous body obeyed her. Then I cried. Deep, soul-wrenching sobs escaped my body. Wendy then put me back together. She held me. Me! I was snot and tears, but she kept holding me. I felt free!

Jenny Vautour, February 2022

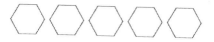

I brought a friend's daughter to True North Revival. For two years, she had seizures all the time, and it was very disruptive to her life. It was disrupting her education and her ability to live. She was really skinny; she didn't eat well for two years because of it.

She had a seizure in the middle of the True North service. So, Tracy, Jane, and I took her to the back room and we prayed for deliverance. God delivered her from some demons, and she got free.

That night wasn't the last time she seized, but it was a dramatic change of less and less and less. Now, she's fully free of them. She's going to university and she's going to be a brain surgeon, as her marks are very high. She must work part-time too. Previously, whenever she had a seizure, she'd be very distracted, and she'd often be sent home by ambulance because she needed to lay down for a few hours. But now she's not seizing at all. Praise God!

Alla Gurevich, October 2022

Financial Testimonies

My husband and I recently started attending The Summit and soon learned that the pastors would often lead a financial declaration before the offering. One morning, I remember standing in church saying the financial declaration and thinking that it would be cool if it happened to us, but honestly kind of doubting whether it ever would.

A week or two later, my husband got an email from his work saying they had a surplus year and to value their employees' hard work, they ran all the staff through an algorithm to factor in the number of years worked, overtime, etc., to determine how much of the surplus each employee could get. We received a very unexpected bonus of $873.10! My husband said his company has never done that in the six years he's worked for them!

My husband has been in school for the past few months to finish his apprenticeship program, and he has been on EI. While we weren't struggling financially, the extra cash before Christmas was such an amazing "God wink" that covered our extra Christmas expenses with some to spare! God is so faithful!

Anonymous, December 2022

We started building our house near Edmonton in April 2021. We had to leave our rental house on April 1, so we chose to save money by living in our travel trailer. When we were framing, the price of the package was about 3 times more than what we had been quoted for, $50,000 more. We ran out of money, so work on the house eventually stopped. We came to the difficult decision to list another house lot we owned in British Columbia in September. Within 24 hours, we had an offer! Unfortunately, about six weeks later, it unexpectedly fell through. No more offers came in as it was too close to winter. We had to live in our travel trailer through the bitterly cold winter with our three kids, which was challenging to say the least, but also a time of closeness for us as a family. My husband did an incredible job of making it warm but it sure was tight quarters!

I started reading the book, *The Invitation* by Tony Stoltzfus in January 2022 and came to the part where I wrote down the top five items I talk about with Jesus. I found that most of them were about things and business, so I asked Jesus what He thought. He told me He cared about me coming to Him with my fears, and told me not to worry, that He had this. He said that He loves talking to me, "No matter what" and He loves filling my desires. God was talking to my husband as well. Two days later, my brother-in-law phoned to say that he and his business partner were going to buy the property! As soon as the finances came through, we were able to continue building our new house. God also provided many people to come alongside us and help. We moved in at the end of October 2022!

Kim de Jong, October 2022

In 1994, I was wearing a halo-vest, after a motor vehicle accident, that left me with a fractured neck in two different places. Following much prayer, fasting, and physiotherapy, I was back a year later in full-time ministry. God was with me then and continued to open doors and prosper our lives and ministry.

Then in 2009, travelling home from Calgary, I got very sick around Red Deer. It took a week for the doctors at the University of Alberta Hospital to discover I had a staph infection, which then morphed into osteomyelitis, which is a bone infection. Osteomyelitis likes to settle in a weak spot in your body, and so it showed up in my previously fractured neck. I literally faced death on a few occasions. During my recovery, I had to be on antibiotics 24/7, for three months, administered through IV. Following that, I continued for three more months on oral antibiotics. The damage that was taking place throughout my neck would become a chronic pain that I would have to endure for the next 12 years. With no other help in sight, and using continued painkillers, I was forced to leave the work I loved and go on medical disability.

Many years later, I heard the story of a hockey player, Jack Eichel, and how he needed a neck surgery after sustaining an injury. With my love of hockey and a player with a neck injury, I paid close attention to his journey. One day, I read a report that Jack Eichel had gone for surgery in Colorado and was doing exceptionally well. I wanted to know what he had done and followed up on the details. I discovered Dr. Chad Prusmack, a renowned neurosurgeon in Denver, Colorado, had done the operation. Dr. Chad is also the team neurosurgical consultant for the Denver Broncos. As a specialist, I don't think I've ever encountered anyone in the medical field that had a more down-to-earth presence, love, and care to see people get better. My daughter, Angeline, and I went down to Denver to have the surgery, then stayed there for two weeks until we were cleared to go back home.

The cost for going was very high, but the cost for not going was even greater. When we heard it was going to cost $65,000 CDN, it was a shock. My daughters came up with the idea of using GoFundMe, an app where money can be raised for various causes. While in the airplane, on our way to Denver, my daughter leaned over to me and said, "Dad, I just checked the GoFundMe account, and there's $65,000 dollars." While in the United States, the exchange rate varied and other miscellaneous expenses occurred, bringing our final expense to $70,000 CDN. Upon our return to Canada, again on the airplane, my daughter leaned over to me again, and said, "Dad, there's $70,224.00 dollars in the account." Tears ran down both our faces, as we sat in awe of our Heavenly Father and His specific care for His children.

I have completed a three-month post-op examination and x-rays, followed by a zoom call with the surgeon, Dr. Prusmack. He is very excited about the healing that's taking place, as the Artificial Disk replacements are lined up perfectly and healing exactly as they should. As only a surgeon could say, when I asked him how it looked, he said, "It was so good, he wasn't sure if he or God had made it that way."

I've been in physical therapy and beginning my third week, post-op. This will go on for the first year, so there's lots of work to be done in order to see the greatest results for the future. To explain how I feel now compared to before surgery is hard to put into words. I could say that my worst day now is better than my best day before. It will take one year for the spinal cord and nerves to reshape and settle into the place they should be. This means it won't be unusual to have set-back days as I rebuild my strength.

Finally, the day I arrived back home, the PA (physician assistant) had left a voicemail on my house phone. He wanted to know if I would be a reference for another gentleman in southern Alberta, which I was so pleased to do. Just three months after my surgery, Dr. Prusmack has operated on six other Canadians!

Ken Solbrekken, June 2022

As a young child growing up, my parents always encouraged me and my siblings to tithe regularly. When the "Tooth Fairy" would come, they would tell me "Remember, this whole toonie isn't fully yours because 10% of it belongs to Jesus".

Or if someone randomly gave me $5 and we were going to the store they would say "Get your $5 but remember 10% of it belongs to

Jesus." This went the same if someone gave me money for my birthday & Christmas or if I got an allowance after doing chores. My parents always drilled it into me growing up, so that as I got older, it became more of a habit.

As an adult, I always tithed regularly, but did it more out of obligation because "We are supposed to give 10% of our finances to God." Sometimes we want to keep our finances to ourselves, especially during times when we're in need. But one thing God has been teaching me lately is that when we tithe, it is actually like a "kingdom investment."

After all the years of giving and giving and giving.. Something powerful happened.

It was the year 2020, right after Covid hit, where God asked me to sign up for this Missions school in the USA, where I would eventually leave from there and head to the Middle East to do some mission / volunteer work overseas. Now at that time, I didn't have any finances (same as most of the people in the world, as we were all put on a "shut down / pause" from work/life/etc). I remember saying to God "This makes no sense. This is crazy, I have nothing. I can't afford to go." But God would always keep telling me "Trust Me. Trust Me." So, I took a step of faith and obedience, signed up and got accepted for the school.

One thing about missions' trips, is usually there is a certain amount of money that is due at a specific time. And I remember weeks or even days prior to the due date, thinking to myself "Okay this is way beyond what I have right now at the moment." Or I would stress and say, "God, I don't know what's going to happen. I don't have this money & they'll probably send me back home." But God always responded with "Do you trust Me?" I would continue to pray and trust that I was in His will, and He would provide the full amount. What amazed me was that every time there was money due on a specific date/ time, it would either be the night before or the day of, where randomly I would get a donation, or the money would appear on my account to cover the full cost. Not only that, but the amount of money needed was in USD dollars. When I would get the CAD dollar amount, & convert it to USD, it would always equal to the exact penny I needed for that day. WOW JESUS!

I remember talking to God and thanking Him each time, and one day He brought back to my memory all the times I would give my 10% to Him. He reminded me of those times I gave even when I was lacking finances. Then I heard him say to me, "Did you know that you weren't just giving because you had to give? You were giving because what you're doing is investing that which I have given you, to be able to do that which I'm calling you to, which seems impossible."

In the span of three months, I had $13,000 CAD provided and all my needs were met on the mission field.

Katelyn Kimo, April 2023

Background data of importance: I was raised in the 90's when the only people who wore masks in North America were bank robbers and bad guys. I entered a workforce where combinations of hoodies, sunglasses, masks, shemagh, and any and all kinds of facial avoidance was a preattack indicator (a sign that some sort of conflict with violence was potentially about to go down).

When Covid lockdown mandate restrictions were at their highest, I had many panic/anxiety attacks. Often, I had to leave the public place that I was in and go home because of the environment.

Location of miracle: East Campus, rear auditorium, foyer access doors.

Timing: The shift between first and second service, as the first congregation leaves and the second congregation comes in.

On the day in question, I was standing at the back in the usher/security role. I was working the double shift, and saying goodbye to those that were leaving and saying hi and trying to help those coming in. Now, there were some people that attended that wore masks, and they were doing it for personal reasons, which I support. Having the medical/tactical knowledge that I have, it bothers/worries me on a personal level; however, my personal feelings don't matter when I'm working. Everyone is given respect and treated fairly and kindly. Disrespect is earned.

I watched a group of people leave. I said goodbye. They responded in kind with conversational pleasantries as they passed by. I had a group of people that walked in and started a conversation with me. As the next group of people walked out, waved, and said goodbye, I answered the group in front of me when suddenly one of the ladies that was leaving was standing in front of me.

Context. This lady was short, grey-haired, and wearing a mask. My brain had a minor flip. I knew she was not a threat, and I knew I shouldn't be having a "moment", but my brain and body were fighting the trained reaction. "Just watch and see what's up," was also trying to go through my brain.

As this lady approached me, she held her hand out, took my hand, and spoke, "This is for you, you aren't to regift it; you aren't to give it to someone; don't use it for anyone but yourself." I was flabbergasted and speechless. I know she said something else, but I was just floored by what she said. I really can't remember if I thanked her.

At that time in my life, I wasn't in a good spot financially. I was making use of various gear bags that really weren't meant for civilian/public areas. Most of what I had left in my life was a personal kit that was multifunctional vis-à-vis areas of operation (military/security roles). I was trying to get a backpack that I could put all my essential day-to-day stuff in, that I could take to church and would be the right fit. However, that cost more money than I could afford. That is until that lady gave me the cost of the bag; I just had to pay for the shipping and import, which I could easily cover.

Now to be clear, I have done what I could in the past with helping people. I grew up being taught the Pentecostal handshake. I had never had a total stranger walk up, hand me a blessing with the direction that *knew me and my habits* to give direction in such a manner. It blew my gourd. It still is awe-inspiring to me. I see that lovely lady who honoured God and His directions come into church practically weekly. If you think I have been able to get over to introduce myself or speak to her, I have to say that it hasn't happened yet. At the time of this writing, I have yet to be able to make it happen. I still don't know her name, or even know what her face looks like. I couldn't pick her out of a lineup if I had to. Professionally this is abysmal; personally, it makes me laugh.

God has a sense of humour and perfect timing. So, that is how I got my Grey Maxpedition Day bag.

Kyle Larade, April 2023

In September of 2021, I just knew the seasons were starting to change in my life.

My post-secondary school was coming up with all these Covid regulations, including mandatory vaccination. They were considering implementing the passport system for the next semester, and I honestly felt relieved because I did not have a vaccine passport. I felt like it would be an easy out to not go. It wouldn't have to be my own decision; it would be made for me.

And when they decided not to implement it, I felt disappointed. I realized I needed to cut back from school. I started by saying, "Okay, I'll take five classes instead of seven. Okay, I'll take four instead of five. Okay, I'll take two. Okay, I'll take one course."

It was like keeping my pinky toe in, just not wanting to walk away entirely. I was still resisting the flow of the Spirit, even though I felt Him leading me away from school.

Finally, God said clearly to me, "Hey, you need to leave. You cannot be here this semester." I said, "Okay, Lord." I began to be obedient.

By the time I had this revelation, I was already past the deadline for payment on that last remaining course. Including all the student fees, I needed to pay $800.

I said, "God, how am I going to pay for a course that I am not going to take? That's so dumb, I'm not gonna do that." So, then I said, "God, clearly, I'm just gonna take the course because I have to pay for it anyway." But the conviction was so strong. God said, "You need to just trust Me." I agreed. I understood He didn't want me to go, and even if I had to pay for the course, I still was not supposed to take it.

I decided to email them. I said, "I just feel like I'm not supposed to be here this year." They replied that it was ok, but my invoice for that one class was sitting there, waiting to be paid. I kept telling myself to go pay it and I was dreading it.

My mom needed to borrow my credit card to order something for someone, and she was going to reimburse me. But in my head, I realized that I would have to wait for the reimbursement before I paid the school.

And then, when the reimbursement was transferred to me, I immediately went to pay for the course.

Two hours before I received the money, someone at the school cleared my balance, completely cleared it. And it wasn't my own academic advisor. It was another VA that didn't even know me or my situation.

I realized that if my mom hadn't put something on my card the day before, I would have paid it. It was crazy. It's why I was able to afford attending the Revival Leadership Institute at The Summit. And I have leftover money too!

I was thinking, what's wise with money in the world, isn't wisdom in God's kingdom. Like, why would you pay for a course that you weren't taking? But God said, "Do it. Trust Me to do it, trust Me do it."

Imagine if I had disobeyed God and taken the course? It probably would have been such a struggle because it would have been against what He wanted. But I obeyed, and He took care of the details, which allowed me to do what He really wanted with that money.

Anonymous, March 2022

Back in February or January 2022, it felt like everything wasn't going right. I was trusting God for a job because the job I was at didn't pay enough to really survive on, and I had no benefits. I felt kind of trapped and I started saying these declarations about finances that we speak at church sometimes. Everything in my life started to go in the opposite direction. I kept hearing stories of people who were being blessed and it would be this little pain in my heart, like a dagger.

Then, I started to try and make things happen on my own. I tried to get a job. I was striving because I felt like I had to generate this testimony about declarations, about my great achievements and it didn't work, and all I got was super frustrated.

I kept getting doors that were shut and I was kind of worried. I'm gonna just use some specific numbers because I need to just tell you how good God is. I thought I was worth another $3,000 to $5,000 per year with maybe a nice vacation, and benefits.

After about three months of wearing myself out trying to find something, I was getting really frustrated. I started to say, "I don't think that God wants me to have a job. I think He wants me to be poor." I started to whine. I said, "If I'm going to be poor, if You want me to stay here in this job, I will serve You. But I quit. I'm done. I'm done trying. I just can't do this anymore."

And that day, I got a call from an agent that I worked with years ago, out of nowhere. She said, "Hey, I don't know if you remember me. We worked together four years ago. I saw your name out of 500 resumes. And I remember that I loved working with you. Do you want to talk? Are you looking for work?" And so, long story short, I spoke with her about everything that I wanted to do. I had this amazing opportunity come up in that moment that opened a door for me to start the interview process.

In the interview, it felt like, "You can't do this, you failed to communicate, you're not gonna qualify, and it's too big for you."

Pastor Chris was actually preaching on favour that week, so I decided to grab hold of that teaching. I said, "Lord, I need favour." I had no business in this particular industry, but I asked God for favour anyways.

And I got the job. There was so much favour. It pays $30,000 more than I was making! Plus 3 weeks vacation, a personal spending account, plus health benefits, and a free gym. God surrounded me with favour!

Anonymous, August 2022

Money is a bit tight right now with two cars, broken windshields, needing tires, and everything. We were only able to afford to get tires put on our Santa Fe and that was like $1,500. We also got the windshield replaced on the car and that was another $500. There were so many expenses. We had just spent $4,000 on flights home to New Zealand and Australia to visit my family that I haven't seen since I moved here.

Someone had a word on the way to church on Saturday night saying someone needed new winter tires. And so, they asked God, "Who, who, who is it?" They found out it was us and transferred us the money we needed to get tires on our other car!

And I feel like it's just a huge testimony to God the whole time we've been here in Canada. He's literally provided every single time. It's just been crazy. People in Australia didn't think we were actually moving here for God. So, coming here and having God show up in miraculous ways is so affirming that we were hearing correctly. Thank You, God.

Rebecca Dunn, November 2022

Rai's Story

In 2020, I was addicted to marijuana, practicing witchcraft, and deeply desiring death in a polyamorous marriage that had once been loving, but was shattered after we lost two children in a car accident. I had been baptized in 2019, but when the Holy Spirit told me to divorce my husband, I slammed the door on God and spiraled into an all-time low.

My husband of nearly ten years had never actually practiced monogamy, so I convinced myself that it was better to stay with him, and at least know about his conquests, than to continue the cycle of catching him in affairs. Soon after that life change, my adoptive mom came down with seven different cancers, many of them at stage four. This was right around the time I found out I was pregnant with my daughter, and she would have an older sister, from a pregnancy my husband was hiding from me. I'd love to say I called out to God, and He saved me there and that my mom was miraculously healed. In a way she was—she renounced paganism and accepted Jesus. She spent her final months encouraging me to walk back towards Jesus. (When I met her, I was a practicing Catholic in an abusive home.) Her dying wish was that all her children would be led to Christ. The truth is I did call out to God, but I never called out to Jesus. I never surrendered my control.

So, a year later, I was grieving my mother, dating a man my husband pressured me to begin a relationship with, and watching my life fall apart more and more every day. My husband rejected me and our daughter, convinced I had somehow cheated on him. Strange occurrences happened daily. Lights flickered, doors slammed, front doors were knocked on with no one there. To this day, I am unshakably convinced that the life I was trapped in was a demonic stronghold. I began having back-to-back dreams of the future; myself calling to me in that moment repeatedly warning myself that the man I was dating was a monster. In those dreams, I often saw myself reading my dusty Bible in a chair, in a church that I now know to be S.H.O.P (Summit House of Prayer) and so, I began reading the word of God again.

After a few weeks in repentance, I kept sensing a dark presence walking through my home. I called my one Christian friend and she declared that she believed there was a demonic presence in the home, and prayed over me that the lies of the enemy would be revealed, that the stronghold on me be broken, and that I would walk in the love of God.

The next day, the man I thought was my fiancé revealed to me that he was a predator and was planning on cheating on me with someone nearly twenty years younger than me. This happened exactly one month after my thirtieth birthday. My life turned upside down. Police were called, parents were notified, and I was thankfully left with no more damage than a lot of broken pieces to pick up. God miraculously opened a door to a new home, and because I was on maternity leave, I spent the following months making the word of God my full-time job. I vowed to be single until He leads me to the husband, I believe He has for me. I promised to get sober, and I decided to radically change everything in my life.

I cut off the polyamorous community, permanently renounced all paganism, and got rid of any witchcraft-related items from my home. I joined prayer groups, Bible studies, found spiritual mentors, and friends. In that year, God undid ten years of damage and brought me back to Him, healing my trauma, saving me from temptation and addiction, and helping me enjoy sobriety and purity. I made mistakes, but I joined a church and was filled with the Holy Spirit, dreams, words of knowledge, and regular signs that lead me on my walk with our Creator.

Coming to The Summit began by hearing God tell me to leave my now previous church. I did not understand where to go but kept getting dreams I knew were from God. I would see the worship team singing, the lobby, the cafe, and True North Revivals. He showed me how to follow Him and led me to The Summit. In truth, I did not want to leave my previous church. I was more than comfortable there; I was egotistical. Being a woman on fire for God in a community that was half asleep meant that I quickly felt like I was superior to others who struggled to suffer for God and lean into a fully surrendered relationship with Him. I, on the other hand, felt entitled, that my history of suffering meant I was deeper with God because I had fully surrendered to Him. That is likely a big part of why He moved me. I was not under leadership that was equipped to position me in a way I could learn. Instead, I was allowed to step into leadership before I was truly in the heart posture I needed to be. I needed to learn to desire others' success more than my own.

Moving to The Summit has been a very humbling and awakening experience for my faith. At my last church, I had received deliverance and learned to hear from God and listen more clearly to His voice. But attending The Summit, I have been learning how to truly love, be loved, serve, and receive from my Father, Christ, and Counselor. Not just to have the Holy Spirit in my life; but to be deeply in relationship, knowing that God Himself is my best friend, lover, guide, leader, father, example, strength, and so much more.

By my second service at The Summit, God had confirmed that this was my home. I, being bitter, decided that it was not the place I was comfortable in, and I did not like it. I was overly critical, and frustrated, mostly at the children's ministry. Our last church had a fantastic children's ministry where I could drop my kids off before worship began and pick them up when I was ready to leave. It was here where God began to challenge me. One of my first times picking up my kids, I looked at the room they had been playing in and was deeply bothered at how unorganized it was (after an hour with MY kids swarming around it like bees; so, bear in mind the real problem here was my attitude). That was where God spoke to me. While I was arguing with Him about how we should go back to our old church, He challenged me to walk into serving this one. He clearly told me, "Instead of being angry at where you think there is a lack, you could serve here and remove the lack," and that, my friends, is how I began volunteering on the cleaning team.

At first, I was bitter, but I realized God was right. I could be angry at the children's ministry and its space for not being what my old church was; or I could invest myself into it, and help it become what it is meant to be. In my strength, I just wanted to drop off my kids and be allowed space from them. But because I submitted to God, I instead began to worship with my children, to explain and teach them the words being spoken, to have a relationship with them, where I became the spiritual leader of our home; not an exhausted single mom who felt entitled to her space from her children.

Leaning into servant leadership on the cleaning team has taught me so much. All that time scrubbing toilets in silence healed my entitled attitude and begin to truly experience joy and gratitude for the many individuals who keep The Summit running well.

I learned to see and identify that which makes The Summit successful are not just the pastors, but in fact its volunteers—the men and women, some of whom volunteer as much as they work at a job. Christians that have a true desire to worship the Lord with their hands and feet; individuals who walk the walk and talk the talk. The volunteers became the family I was agonizing over not having. For the first time in over a decade, I felt my iron was being sharpened, my theology challenged, my foundation rooted in more than just excited ramblings, but real concrete unshakable convictions. Instead of feeling overly confident and entitled in a community that struggled to read their Bible daily, I was rapidly growing in my understanding of who God is in a community that confirms the beliefs I was developing and leads from humility, not judicial convictions.

Since joining the cleaning team, I have been privileged to witness many wonders. I saw my own heart accept the love of God. The once dead joyous person inside I had believed buried with my children was resurrected into abounding energy and zeal for servanthood and inspiring others to desire impact for His kingdom. I have been in constant wonder at the healing my heart has been able to receive and give. My relationship with my biological parents went from nonexistent after a decade of pain, to speaking with both, and one of my parents is actively now in a deep relationship with the Holy Spirit.

My dad flew across the country to witness my son be baptized this year. My children pray, my house is set free, and God has continued to work miracles in my finances, housing, pets, friendships, healing in my body, and mind. I have been blessed to serve and in this season of serving, I have finally been able to attain the peace I always wanted, the love I could never find, the hope I thought long dead, and the joy I believed would only ever come tomorrow.

Rachel (Rai) Dixon, July 2023

Jen's Story

"Yes, ma'am, it's very clear," the doctor said in broken Japanese-English. "The tumor is visible right here," pointing to the MRI image on the screen in front of us. As my husband, James, and I looked at each other, we knew things were going to change. I also felt relieved to finally have a clear diagnosis after two years of confusion and sickness. At that moment, I had no idea what the future would hold.

Let me go back to the beginning. My story, and God's triumph, are not well explained without going back. So, bear with me as I walk you through my health journey over the last six years.

September 2017 - I realized my weight had been slowly increasing over the last year or so. I was now 180 lbs and climbing. I had started a job that was fairly fast-paced and stressful, and my stress eating had gotten out of hand. I didn't want to follow my "genetic path" with weight. I have a lot of type 2 diabetes in my family, and I wanted to break that cycle. I joined Orange Theory Fitness (OTF) to work at getting stronger and more fit. I was going three times per week consistently and working out hard. I found I was getting stronger, I could work out longer, and not be in as much pain the next day.

By Christmas that year, I had not seen much change in my physique or my weight. I determined that I needed to make some food changes as well. On New Year's Day 2018, I started Weight Watchers. I stuck to the plan and the point structure for 3 months. I was very strict with myself and still attended OTF three times per week. I really did not want to pass the genetic predisposition down to my kids. I knew that if I didn't change my habits, my kids wouldn't be set up well for success. After three months I still had not seen any weight change.

March 2018 - For my birthday, my friend, Mark, and I went downhill skiing at Lake Louise. It was such a beautiful day! I felt stronger than I had in a long time. I was really excited to ski from open to close on our day trip to the mountains! Unfortunately, by lunch time, even with multiple rest breaks, my legs were not able to keep me up anymore. I don't remember ever feeling that kind of pain in my calves! I wondered whether my technique had changed a lot since I ski instructed. Was I so out of practice that I was hurting myself? I couldn't understand what I had done that caused so much pain. I could not carry my equipment to the car. Mark helped carry everything. He even helped lift my legs into the car after I limped my way over. I tried to stay positive and joyful. I just thought I had overdone it.

I continued with OTF, but seeing as nothing had changed with Weight Watchers, I made some more changes. I tried keto and clean eating. I went off processed sugar, flour, dairy, gluten, and all other processed food. Even with all of that, I was gaining weight. I was still attending OTF three times per week and maintaining my strict diet. It was amazing how simple it was to do it when I was faced with hard health challenges. It was so maddening though that I was still gaining weight!

April 2018 - At that point, my work had changed to "commission only" which added to my stress. I was not coping with everything physically and I was not performing well enough in sales. I found I could not keep up with the demands and quotas, and I was regularly on an emotional roller coaster. I was also worried about money.

My husband, James, had downsized a lot of his business, and I was the major breadwinner. My income paid our bills and kept food in the fridge. During the major diet changes to keto and clean eating, I was also working full time and figuring out our finances. We decided to refinance our house and pull money out of the equity. Given my personality, I never seem to do anything part way. We renovated the house to get the most amount we could from the refinance. I have to tell you I yelled and screamed and cried at God regularly! I didn't know if I would get a paycheck. I didn't know how we were going to pay the bills. I was working full time and then coming home to renovate for 6+ hours each night. I often cried myself to sleep.

At that point, I was 2 years into my faith walk with God and feeling absolutely out of depth. I looked around to my prayer sisters and all I could think is, "Yeah, but you guys have history with God! You have experience that tells you He will carry you through. I DON'T HAVE THAT!" James also applied to work at the City of Edmonton as an electrical inspector. We hadn't heard back yet if he had got the position.

May 2018 - I went to see my family doctor for blood work because nothing I was doing was making a difference. "Maybe something is wrong medically?" When the results came back, he told me, "Everything is in normal ranges. Keep doing what you're doing, and the weight should come off."

June 2018 - I was in a daily grind. I was getting up and pushing myself to work when I felt hopeless. I would get home and coordinate the kids, make dinner in the makeshift kitchen, and spend the evening finishing the renovations. I was exhausted, and all I could do was yell at God, "Why am I here? What am I supposed to do? How do we get through this?" We finished the reno at the end of June. It felt wonderful to have it completed! Yet, the financial pressure was growing, so the process of filing for refinancing began. It was a trying time of waiting. I really had no words to describe how I felt every day. I was just a daily ball of stress. I had stopped working out at OTF as we couldn't afford the rates. I was stumped on my weight. Nothing I was doing was working and I didn't know why.

August 2018 - God came through! The financing was approved on our mortgage, and we had money in the bank to pay bills. What a relief, especially because I was just laid off. I got to enjoy my summer. I planned to look for work again in September when the kids went back to school. We heard back on the job for James, and he had been offered the position with the City. He started in September, and we really felt like we could breathe again. He was now making the most money he had ever made at a position. The position had good hours, good holiday time, and benefits. We had some money in the bank and things were looking really good. Our family dynamics were good. However, I was still putting on weight like it was going out of style.

I decided I would go see a naturopath because my medical doctor said everything was fine. "Maybe something was missed." When I saw the Naturopath, she pulled up my bloodwork. She said my cortisol (stress hormone) was at the very high end of normal. My testosterone was also above the normal ranges. I was so frustrated! My family doctor hadn't even scheduled a follow-up for the bloodwork. The Naturopath showed me a list of symptoms and asked if I thought it covered everything I was experiencing. I was astonished that I had ninety percent of all the symptoms, including rare ones. She gave me some supplements to reduce my cortisol, hoping that I was just experiencing adrenal fatigue. The Naturopath said I needed to see an endocrinologist (hormone specialist) about my high cortisol and that I needed blood work redone to see if her suspicion of Cushing's disease was correct. I went back to my family doctor to get the referral to the specialist. I was also scheduled for an MRI to check for a tumor, which could be the cause of Cushing's disease.

October 2018 - I went for the MRI and saw the endocrinologist. She said there was nothing visible on the MRI and that the supplements I was taking for the adrenal fatigue were actually likely *causing* my high cortisol. My cortisol was now well over the high limit in my most recent blood work. I was told to stop taking all the supplements for thirty days and then repeat my blood work. My strength overall seemed to be decreasing quickly. The charley horses in my legs happened more often and were more painful. I also realized that I had swelling in my hands. I took my wedding rings off because they were so tight that the skin was getting rashes underneath them.

October 23, 2018 - James was in a very bad car accident that was not his fault. Thank God the kids weren't with him. The collision totaled our minivan. There was enough force in the collision that the replacement car battery we had in the back of the van actually broke open on the seats from the force, spraying battery acid all over the carpet and seats. I was so very grateful it hit the seats and not my husband!

December 2018 - I had my follow-up call with the endocrinologist after my blood work results had come in. She said, "Since you have come off the supplements, your cortisol is now within the normal range again. This means you do not have Cushing's disease as I expected".

"So, what is causing my weight gain then?" I asked.

"There are many causes of obesity. I do not know what might be causing yours. I do know that it is not Cushing's disease. Maybe you could consider going to the Obesity Clinic? They might have more answers or solutions to your weight issues."

"What about the sweating, hair growth, swelling, and trouble walking? What about the rest of my symptoms? Aren't there more tests to do?" I asked.

"You were referred to me to determine if you had Cushing's disease. I have determined that you do not. It's not really my job to figure out the rest. I don't have any more tests to run for you. Good luck," she said.

I got off the phone thinking, "She basically just told me to go to the Obesity Clinic to get my stomach stapled to resolve my weight gain. What about everything else? Where on earth do I go from here?!"

I also realized my sleep was affected. I had insomnia and had trouble waking up in the morning. I was exhausted all the time. My doctor sent me for a sleep apnea test. I ended up getting a sleep apnea machine. I was pretty sure my sleep apnea was due to my increased weight. I became desperate and depressed. I went to a private hormone clinic. They told me I had polycystic ovarian syndrome, that there is no cure, and to try intermittent fasting. I wasn't convinced.

January 2019 - I went to a private medical doctor. He did the largest blood panel I had had to date. 26 vials. I thought, "If he doesn't find anything, then what?!" While I was awaiting results from all the tests, I had a four-day period where I gained ten pounds! "How is it physically possible to gain ten pounds in four days?!" I felt awful. I couldn't sleep. I felt like I was choking on myself if I laid down. My neck and face were so swollen. I had swelling in my legs. I had red stretch marks all over my stomach, arms, breasts, and legs, which is a typical Cushing's symptom. I felt like no one was seeing what I was living through. I couldn't reach above my head with both my arms, otherwise I would literally choke myself. I decided to go to the emergency room.

Over the next few weeks, I went in and out of the ER multiple times. The staff all believed that I had Cushing's disease given my symptoms. I was referred to two different endocrinologists, so I had multiple opinions. One of them listened well and saw what I was going through. She admitted me to the hospital to fast track some testing. I was seen by internal medicine specialists to make sure I didn't have heart issues. I had everything tested that could be tested. Everything was pointing back to a tumor causing Cushing's disease. "How!? I have an MRI that shows no tumor?" The endocrinologist that specializes in Cushing's disease was currently in Japan at a conference. I needed to go for another MRI. Apparently, there are different settings for the MRI machine to see smaller things. I waited for him to get back, so that the settings could be arranged, and only have to do the MRI once properly. In mid-February, I went for the new MRI with proper settings, in the newest machine, and with contrast.

March 1, 2019 - James was in another terrible car accident. It was also not his fault. It was another car totalled and we had to shop for a new one just 4 months after the last one. He also sustained more injuries. Because I was going through my own medical nightmare, I was unable to see and understand James' injuries and trauma.

March 8, 2019 - "Yes, ma'am, it's very clear," the doctor said in broken Japanese-English, "The tumor is visible right here." I was so glad to have a clear diagnosis, yet, I was so scared about what it meant. I was pretty certain through my research the result would be brain surgery. It turned out that I had a rare type of Cushing's, called Cyclical Cushing's disease. There are only a few ways a person can get Cushing's disease, which causes too much cortisol in the body. It can come from steroid use, alcoholism, and tumors. Tumors can be in the brain on the pituitary gland, which produces ACTH. ACTH triggers your adrenal glands to produce cortisol. Tumors can also be on your adrenal glands causing them to malfunction. It is very rare, but tumors can also grow anywhere in your body. If the tumor itself is creating and secreting the ACTH hormone, this would also cause Cushing's disease. Cushing's disease is the most complicated endocrine disorder, making it like the proverbial needle in a haystack to diagnose. My tumor was growing inside my pituitary gland. It was squishing the gland from the inside out, which is why it wasn't visible on the first MRI. That is also why I was experiencing the other hormonal issues of sweating, hair growth, monthly cycle issues, and swelling. The tumor itself was also creating and secreting the ACTH hormone. This is what caused the change in my cortisol levels and why it was sometimes within the normal ranges and sometimes high. That's why it's called "Cyclical Cushing's".

My symptoms were *all* a result of Cushing's disease. It finally explained my significant weight gain, swelling, insomnia, muscle and joint pain, bright red stretch marks, fatigue, and emotional turmoil. High cortisol levels put the body into "fight or flight" mode. This causes digestive system malfunction, fluid retention, muscle deterioration, insomnia, and mood swings. My final diagnosis was Benign Pituitary Adenoma causing Cyclical Cushing's disease. I virtually became an expert on this disease. Statistically, Cushing's disease is ten in a million. Cyclical Cushing's disease is two in a million. I hated being a medical anomaly.

It was a full month before I was seen by the neurosurgeon. During that month, the doctor put me on a number of medications for pain, swelling, and also to try to get the tumor to shrink. All of the meds had side effects, but I didn't care. Things had gotten so bad that I was sleeping in a Lazyboy recliner on my main floor because I couldn't make it up the stairs. I couldn't stand long enough to make dinner. It was sketchy showering as I felt unstable. I was even using a walker in our home, so I was willing to try anything.

When I did see the surgeon, I was informed that I did need brain surgery. "Heaven help me!" I had so many questions that the appointment was over an hour long. The biggest question I had was, "How soon can I have the surgery?!"

"There are only four people per month that can have this particular surgical procedure done. There are only so many days the four different specialties involved in it can all be in the same place at the same time. You are on the list, and you're considered urgent due to the severity. I know it won't be this month (April) as those slots are already scheduled. We will keep you posted as more information becomes available regarding scheduling," the surgeon told us.

"Wonderful." I thought between the various swear words going through my mind.

May 2019 - I woke up one morning to every stretch mark in my mid-section having hives in the soft part of the stretched skin. It was all consuming and so painful. I went back to the ER. "What am I allergic to?" I was sent to a dermatologist. It took another week to be able to see him. More testing determined that I was having an allergic reaction to T3's, one of the painkillers I was taking. I was given heavy antihistamines and a special cream to put on everywhere. It took weeks for the hives to settle. I only really got relief when I put ice packs on so I couldn't feel anything. I think I called the surgeon's office to find out about dates and scheduling every two days. I was becoming friends with the administrator.

June 3, 2019 - I finally got the call! I was going for surgery in two weeks! I don't like looking at odds, and yet, there I was looking at odds. Brain surgery has come a really long way. They were literally going to do the surgery through the back of my nose, instead of a giant hole in the side of my head. I still did not know whether I was going to come out of surgery. If I did, would I be better or worse than before? Not knowing the answers to those questions makes you do some big things when you have a family. We pulled our kids from school and went to Mexico for a week. This trip was possibly the "last family vacation" we would go on together. The kids were 9 and 11 years old at the time.

Mexico was wonderful and horrible at the same time. Swelling gets so much worse in the heat! "Wheelchair Accessible" in Mexico is different than it is in Canada. I still have amazing memories of our time there. We intentionally set aside time to pray as a family and speak about important things. At the same time, the kids were young, and they didn't really understand everything that was happening. We wanted to have fun and laugh and play as much as possible. After we got home, I actually wrote goodbye letters that I hoped I would never have to give out.

June 17, 2019 - Surgery Day - I went in that day weighing 293 lbs. Interestingly, I don't remember a lot from that day. My most vivid memory is wheeling from my room on the ward to the surgical wing. I was one of the first in the surgical waiting room. I watched as the room filled with others and then emptied again. A nurse finally said, "There you are," like they had lost where they put me. The whole time I was waiting and being prepped in the surgical suite, I was singing 'I Surrender All' in my head. As a million things were happening around me, I was singing inside and trying to convince myself that

I was *actually* surrendering. I silently cried and prayed that I would wake up on the other side.

When I did wake up (hallelujah!), I couldn't open my eyes and I was disoriented and in pain. When James held my hand, I couldn't wrap my fingers around his. My hands were so swollen. My feet felt like they were about to tear apart from swelling. It turns out the anesthetist gave me cortisol during surgery. It's standard practice during surgery so our bodies can handle the stress. But a Cushing's patient already has too much cortisol, so they aren't supposed to give you extra. It made all my symptoms jack to a whole other level. After surgery for the first twenty-four hours, I wasn't allowed to sit up. Any change in pressure can cause problems to the surgical site. Making it through those first hours and days took absolutely everything in me to surrender and trust God. I had to continue having faith and not give up. What a challenge.

In the five days I was in the hospital before going home, I lost fifteen pounds in fluid. I was already able to see major changes in my face and swelling. Truly at this point, I had already experienced a miracle. Medically speaking, the equipment didn't exist to be able to see my tumor even thirty years ago. They definitely didn't have the surgical ability to complete this procedure. I would have died even one generation ago, and without a diagnosis. Just *that* alone is a miracle from God. He used the hands and feet of believers and unbelievers alike for my miracle.

Over the summer, I progressively got better with more movement, walking, and sleeping. The brain surgery recovery was an eight-week process. Cushing's recovery was much, much longer. I was dependent on prednisone because my body's feedback loop was skewed after removing the tumor. If I didn't take the medication, my body would go into shock and die. But I was losing weight and feeling stronger. I had a glimmer of hope that life could go on. I still had no idea what it would look like long term or if I would ever work again.

October 2019 - In conversations with James, I came to realize that I was getting better, but he was not. Looking back, I could see that he put all of his injuries and trauma from the car accidents into a compartmentalized box. Being worried whether his wife would die, and he would become a single parent, meant he did not care about his own injuries. He saw specialists and went for testing. He had pain in his neck, back, shoulder, and knee. He was very light and sound sensitive. He was placed on concussion protocol, which was a dark room with no screens or brain stress for a week. He was also put on short-term disability. Our roles were now reversed. I was actually the "better" one. James was off work until February of 2020. During that time, we realized we needed to sell our rental property. It had been vacant, and we couldn't manage it anymore. We also became aware that a two-storey home was not a good choice long term for us medically. So, we listed both properties and started looking for a bungalow.

March 12, 2020 - We got possession of our "new to us" bungalow. Getting this house was truly God produced. Our rental property sold, but the new family wouldn't take possession until April. Our current house hadn't sold yet, but there were showings, so we were hopeful.

March 14, 2020 -The world shut down and Covid-19 hit Edmonton. "Okay God. You have gotten us this far. Somehow, we have this house when we shouldn't. James is back to work and seems okay. I am getting better every day. But the world is shut down and somehow, I OWN THREE HOUSES!" There were three weeks of lots and lots of prayer and stress. The rental sale did progress, and we were down to just two properties. Through Covid, we were able to defer some mortgage payments and do some renovations. Somehow, God made it possible. I still don't really know how we physically did it. We even lived in a tent in the backyard when the renos weren't yet completed. It was nice to have fewer properties and less bills. It wasn't going to get any easier though. My CPP disability was declined, and I had to appeal. Who knew if it would ever be approved.

2020-2022 - To condense things, the next two years were a blur. In some ways I was better, but in others not. James was working but it wasn't a good situation. Eventually, he had to stop working and return to disability. If I thought our finances were tight before I got sick, it was nothing compared to this season. Now that our roles were reversed, I developed a better understanding of how James felt while I was sick. Being the supporter, while I couldn't make him better, was frustrating. I was learning how to pray and give James and his healing to God too. The kids turned into teenagers, which came with its own challenges. When two parents aren't well, it definitely takes a toll on everyone. I had no idea where our lives were going. I felt depressed because there was no end in sight; physically, emotionally, financially, relationally, with kids and in my marriage. "Logically, I know You are here, and You never leave me, but I don't see You, Lord."

*Definition of a **Come to Jesus moment(s)**: A moment of sudden realization, comprehension, or recognition that often precipitates a major change.*

April 10, 2022 - I was looking forward to seeing my friend, Melissa, at Boston Pizza after church. I hadn't really spoken to her since before Covid and so much in life had happened. I was thinking of all the things I wanted to say. I was doing better since my brain tumor was removed. I had lost some weight, but I had plateaued at 205 lbs for the last 2 months. James was not doing well and had not recovered from his car accidents. The traumatic brain injury (TBI) and compounded concussions were very compli-cated. His physical injuries were also painful and chronic by then. Given both of our medical treatments and decreased income with both of us not working, managing our finances had become more than challenging. I also didn't really know how to support the kids. Keira was 13 and Riley was 11 and we were under pressure from so many places. I had even just pulled Keira out of school to homeschool, which has its own pressures. We couldn't seem to get any reprieve!

I arrived first and settled into the booth. I made a pact with myself that I wouldn't take over the whole conversation for a pity party, and I'd make space for Melissa to share as well.

I gave her a hug and she said, "God has some things to say to you today! I brought my journal and Bible and I've been praying about today since we booked this."

Seven hours later, we walked out of Boston Pizza. I had pages of notes in my phone and felt wrung out from emotions and a litany of things in my head to process. I knew it was an important meeting and had lots to think about. Looking back, I can see it clearly as my "Come to Jesus moment".

One of the first things I actively pursued from that *moment* was looking for a church closer to our home. We had been driving 45 minutes each way to church on Sundays for the last 7 years. We needed a church community that was closer to home that we could tie into more regularly. We needed to be able to connect and the drive time and fuel costs were stopping us from that.

Over the next four days, I opened Google maps and started clicking on any church close to our home. It didn't matter what denomination it was. I clicked and started reading what they were about and their philosophy. I listened to sermons if they were available. I just kept clicking and moving on until I clicked on The Summit Edmonton. After listening to one sermon from the podcast and bawling my eyes out, I knew we needed to go see what it was all about.

On Good Friday, our family attended our first service at Summit. Having never been there, we were surprised by the announcement at the beginning that they would be showing scenes from "The Passion" during the service. I was crying shortly into the service. Keira left to go to the kids' room about halfway through. Riley snuggled into James' shoulder and stopped watching at some point. I was wrecked and felt cracked open by the experience there. I was moved and saw the crucifixion in a new way. God loved me enough to go through *that*! As we got into the car, James turned to me and said, "We are never going back there."

From the emotions of the service, our family spent the rest of the evening fighting. I told James, "We need to give it a chance. One service doesn't tell us enough." We did end up going back on Easter Sunday. Looking back, I can see it as the beginning of this important chapter in my life.

April-July 2022 - What a whirlwind! My weight dropped for the first time in months after starting thyroid medication. It was the first small move in the right direction. I was getting to know myself and God as I heard about beloved identity. I had so many questions! What does beloved identity mean? Does it really apply to me? If God really does love me, why am I living through such a deep, dark, lightless valley? When does it end? Does my life ever get better? This battle has been furious, long, and it seems there is no end. How do I reconcile my experiences with Abba Father, Daddy, and this beloved identity that I don't feel? I am longing for a deeper relationship with my Abba. I feel completely lost and broken.

How do I begin to explain the spiritual changes in my heart and mind and the hard questions I had to ask God? Were there things in my own mind and history that I had to challenge? I understood, "There is tension between hearing the Lord's promise over my life and circumstances and holding that promise in reality." What if I didn't need tragedy to push me into constant prayer? What would my life look like with God then? How do I avoid the trap of striving?

Biblical definition of Miracle: *An event that involves the direct and powerful action of God, transcending the ordinary laws of nature and defying common expectations of behavior.*

If I *could* create an outcome through my own strength or ability, by definition, it literally could not be a miracle of God. I was trying to heal my body, fix James, and move forward in my life using my own strength. It wasn't working. It was also exhausting trying to do it all on my own. I thought, "God must be punishing me," or, "What do I need to learn so God can stop this test?"

June 11, 2022 - School of Intercession - I had a guided experience of Jesus walking me to the throne room of God. In that moment, I could feel His warmth. I laid my head in His lap. I felt His hand on my head like my daddy used to do when I was young. As I was struggling through my many thoughts, I heard God say, "Jen, you don't need to know how to do this. I will give you your next steps, in time." I found a corner of the room to lay down as I cried. I felt the need to surrender but didn't know how to begin. I breathed deeply and intentionally relaxed every muscle in my body. I let the floor support my body. Time evaporated. I opened my hands as I imagined releasing my thoughts and worries and physically laying them down at His feet. I continued to cry but felt a sense of peace when my hands were open and not holding onto "it" anymore. I put my hands behind my head like I was laying in the bow of a ship. "Jesus, You guide my boat. I'm letting go."

Somehow, I got it in my head that God expects a daily performance from me. I always felt like I was "not enough" or that I had to "do" something to be loved by God. Maybe that is my human response to this world. Maybe it was from various experiences growing up. However, I would never treat my kids like I was believing God was treating me! How did I get so mixed up? Logically, I understood that God loves me just as I am, without doing anything. And yet, somehow, I struggled with this every single day.

July 2022- The Altar, Drayton Valley- I only heard about The Altar the previous Sunday, and somehow everything worked out for us to attend. I was grateful that there was no fee expected or we could not have attended. We slept in a tent in a field. We ate under a big tent with 1,800 other people. I was astonished with the amount of people in the middle of nowhere Alberta. The worship was unbelievable, and God's presence was tangible. I watched my daughter Keira experience Him in such a joyful way at the altar crying, laughing, and dancing with Jesus. She changed, and her path shifted that weekend. Keira and I were baptized in water together with 200 other people. I felt called to release some things to God and lay them at His feet on the altar.

"God, I leave money and the choices around it to You. I leave paying the bills and all the stress to You. I am not the provider, You are. I give You my terrible history with money decisions. I will wait on You for steps, and let You decide how and when the money YOU provide should be spent. I pray You refine this part of me. Make it acceptable to save. Take my desires to spend away. Make it so my yearning is for You alone. I also leave James and his healing journey to You. I don't know Your timing Lord and I don't understand it. I lay it at Your feet."

At the end of the weekend, we heard about another gathering in northern Alberta 10 days later. It was over the weekend of Keira's birthday. As we were driving home, Keira informed me that she had already signed up to attend. If I didn't want to go with her, she would find her own way there. She was only 13 at the time! "Who am I to keep my daughter from seeking the Lord?" I thought. After juggling things, and her agreeing to spend her birthday money on gas to get us there, we attended 'It Is Time Canada 2022'.

The first night, I had such a sweet moment with Jesus during worship. We sang, "It's Your Breath in My Lungs." I realized it truly is His breath in my lungs. "I'm here! I'm here after brain surgery! Thank You, Jesus!" I felt His arms wrap around me from behind in a warm hug. I heard Him whisper, "Child, you are worthy of rest and peace. Why is it that when I try to give it to you, you refuse My gift?" I broke open. I had been yearning and crying out for peace and calm for years. That day, I realized all I had to do was accept what He had been trying to give me all along. I started wondering: how much can I be consumed by God on any given day? What am I putting my attention on? When I am seeking comfort, do I run to Jesus, or do I fill it with food, alcohol, or general busyness? I walked away from that weekend feeling so very grateful that I have a strong daughter that "forced" me to go!

August 2022- The very next weekend True North Revival (TNR) at Summit - Over the last few months, my doctor had me reducing my prednisone medication. There are major side effects of coming off that medication. For me, it was a slow and painful process. Every time I reduced my meds, even a little bit, I would become easily fatigued, lethargic, emotionally unstable, and every bone in my body ached. It also caused emotional problems in our home and made my life miserable. With James also not being well, I was constantly stressed on top of everything else. "Should I be doing this? Should I just stay on the meds? If I do, will I be forever dependent on them? If I keep trying to reduce them, will the pain get worse? Can my family handle this? Will my kids and husband survive?" I was exhausted. I stayed in bed all day sleeping on and off just to attend the evening service. Every joint was in pain; everything felt swollen and hurt to move.

During worship, I stood at the front barely moving. After last weekend, I knew God could meet me even in my pain, so I stayed engaged. Worship had become a space to meet God in, so I didn't want to miss Him. I prayed for deeper connection with Him. I asked for my pain to leave and God to fill me with His presence and peace. Mostly, I just cried in pain.

At the end of worship, Pastor TJ Green asked, "Who here is burnt out? Who is in spiritual leadership and is feeling burnt out?"

I was the spiritual leader in our home at that moment. James was still dealing with his chronic pain. As much pain as I was in, I was still the "better" one between us. So, I raised my hands. I felt hands on my back, from those around me, praying over me.

"I feel like God wants to heal adrenal insufficiency," said TJ.

I burst into tears. I thought to myself, "Are you seeing me right now, Lord? Please heal me!"

During offering, I got this quiet voice in my head saying, "I've got you. Don't take your meds tomorrow morning."

Whaaaaat?? "Wait, I could barely get out of bed today, and I'm just on *reduced* medication. What will happen if I stop them all together?! What do you mean just don't take any?" Everything I have read about coming off prednisone is DON'T do it cold turkey!

"Wait! Trust, trust, trust, trust, trust..." I repeated in my head. "If all else fails, I guess it's Saturday and I can just stay in bed all day." This is how I justified this crazy thought to myself.

"Ok Jesus, I won't take anything. But I'm not telling anyone just in case this is me thinking crazy thoughts and it's not You at all!" I said to myself.

The message that night: Mark 4:35 Jesus calms the storm.

They cried in the parable, "Do you not care we are perishing?" I realized I do this in my prayers when my timeline doesn't seem to match God's. I keep forgetting He is in my boat with me! He has me even when I feel crushed by the storm.

"Sometimes when it seems illogical is when it is MOST logical to God."

Trials also create an opportunity for me to grow and increase my belief. Not just for me, but for the "other little boats" (people), watching as I live my life with Jesus in MY boat. How will I respond to my challenges? With peace, joy, and love? The "other little boats" are watching me, to see if I will respond like I have the Creator of the heavens and earth in my boat with me or not. Do I believe?

The sermon was a direct challenge on whether I would trust Him and have faith in miracles.

On a normal day, I would have set an alarm for 4 a.m. to roll over and take my prednisone, then go back to sleep. That way I was able to wake up fully between 8 or 9 a.m.; however, that day, I consciously did not set an alarm the night before to take my meds. I *chose* faith. I crawled into bed after church tired and in pain.

I woke up by myself at 9:30 a.m.! "I can't believe I'm awake! I didn't take the meds!" As I walked to the bathroom, I realized my feet didn't hurt! I unrolled the toilet paper, and my hands didn't hurt! "Ok," I thought, "We will see if it lasts." I decided to take Keira shopping at Chapters that morning. We walked around the store for about 2 hours. "My back doesn't hurt." Wait, what?!?!

Then I took Keira to take her learner's test for driving, which she unfortunately failed. This resulted in a huge breakdown. I spent time talking with her and really heard her and encouraged her. I didn't lose my cool back with her! "Wait, wait, wait, that's not what normally happens!" I thought to myself. I felt like I was in a dream. How could this be real?

I took the kids to their cousins in the afternoon to give James a break. I decided to stay for dinner because I still had energy somehow! I was even able to help clean up after dinner. There was TNR again that night, so we dropped Riley off at home with James, and Keira and I left for church. On the way, I told Keira I hadn't taken meds that day. I had not told anyone yet. She totally freaked out in a good way and couldn't believe it! After replaying everything I had done that day, her mind was blown. When we got to church, I was able to share with Pastor Chris Frost what had happened since the night before. He asked me to share after worship. I jumped and sang and worshiped loudly. WITH NO PAIN! I had been busy ALL DAY and didn't need to sleep yet. And I had not taken any meds!

The message Saturday night:

1. Stay in a state of expectation daily. What are we going to do together today, Jesus?

Walk on water moments happen. Matthew 14:29.

I must be willing to step out of the boat to experience them. "Well, that seems to be true today!" I had to be willing to go without the meds and risk it.

2. Expect painful stretching.

Stop trying to run from what hurts. Embrace it. Stop trying to win wars that only WORSHIP can win. I realized that most of my big breakthroughs come during worship!

3. Time is the test. Prov 17:3 How can I trust a leader if they haven't gone through "breaking" times? *"The Lord tests the heart."*

If I can't do it on my own, it's usually an indicator that God's working.

I finally got a chance to tell James on Sunday afternoon that I hadn't taken medication since FRIDAY! The expression on his face was hilarious. "Is this how God feels when He watches us experience His wonders?"

The next test would be if my medical professionals saw a change in my blood work and whether my next scans would be clean. When they looked at all my blood work, EVERYTHING was in normal ranges. I sat back in my chair and thought, "Wow! He really did it!" I had a moment's hesitation when I went for my next MRI. "Maybe it's back? Maybe it was just some reprieve?" And yet, at the next doctor appointment, I was still tumor free! Medically speaking, there is always a chance for it to regrow, if even one cell was left behind after surgery. Because of the severity of my condition, I will continue to be monitored by specialists in some fashion for the rest of my life. Even knowing that, I no longer have the level of anxiety or fear that I used to have. God healed me! Not in the time I would have liked, not before I had experienced the pain of the experience and not before financial hardships. And still, I am healed! In a moment, God took care of everything I had been asking for. He did it literally overnight.

So, what is different for me now? I believe things are possible. Where before I might have said, "I don't want to get my hopes up," now I say, "I can keep hoping because I have seen what He can do." I went to get some photos done within the first month after His healing. It was special because we did it at sunrise. Previously, sunrise was a "never happening" kind of thing because I couldn't wake up properly. I am so glad I "memorialized" this miracle in my life. I now have printed photos around my house from that day. It helps me stay present to the goodness after the storm and that the possibilities are endless. God is on my side even when things feel bleak. I can choose to look at all the areas in my life, at this moment, that are still in the valley. I can also choose to look at the light, the sunrise, the smiles, and the peace. Every day is a day I can reset and rechoose. Do I fail and get sucked into the dark some days? Does life overwhelm me still? Yes! The difference now is that I have the life experience that it truly can change in a moment! Do I still question God's timing and hope that today looks different? Sure! My husband is still dealing with head injuries, physical trauma, PTSD, depression, and chronic pain (at least at the time I am writing this). I can now hold hope for James' healing to happen overnight, just like mine. And if God healed me, then He *is* capable of healing James. While writing this, I am under financial pressure like I have never experienced. Yet, I still manage to pay my bills and have food on my table. His provision has been astonishing. Today, my body is stronger than it has been since 2017. I wake up on my own.

I don't know why God chooses different timing for different people. I am living in the middle of that question mark every day in my own home. I *know* that God loves me. I *know* He wants only the best for me, just as I love and want the best for my children. I don't know why "bad things happen to good people". I can, however, say with confidence and certainty that I *have* experienced God's presence and peace. I have felt His healing. I have even felt His arms around me, in a tangible hug, when I was standing alone in worship. In the midst of incredible adversity, pressure, and uncertainty, I *know* God is for me.

Guess what! If God is for me and if He can do everything I listed, it means He is also for YOU! My prayer, Lord, is this...

Let everyone that reads this have an opening in their mind and spirit. Lord, because You have shown it's possible in my life, let them see it as possible in their own lives. That they don't buy into the lies that they need to "Do" or "Be" something different to receive Your peace. That if they touch this book, You will open their mind to new possibilities. That You would flood them with peace that belies their current experience.

That they can live their life every day and still know that You are in their boat, just as You are in mine. I pray for hope to reignite and for blessings and provision to flow. I pray that even in the struggle, they will choose faith. That when You whisper to them, they choose to act on it, even when they think it might be crazy! I pray they know how very, very loved they are. Amen!

Jen Garrison, July 2023

2015   2019   2023

The Summit Edmonton Church

In 2009, Chris and Nikki Mathis planted Fresh Anointing House of Worship in Crestview, Florida, USA. In 2013, the organization name was changed to The Summit. It began to expand with other churches and ministries being planted, as well as many becoming affiliated with The Summit.

In 2017, Pastors Chris and Nikki took three churches, River City Church of Edmonton, Fresh Oil & Fire Apostolic Church, and Revival Family Gathering, that were all connected to The Summit, and merged them to become one new church, The Summit Edmonton Church in Edmonton, Alberta, Canada.

Chris and Nikki felt called to come to Canada to pastorally lead this church. It has grown substantially since then, and has seen countless salvations, healings, and miracles.

Chris and Nikki, through their partner ministry, Summit Global Ministries - Edmonton, oversee churches across Canada, the USA, and Brazil, as well as The Summit Edmonton Church. They continue to have a heart for church planting, and they look forward to seeing revival stretch across the world.

The core values of The Summit Edmonton Church are Family, Devotion, Revival, and Hope.

Find us at www.thesummitchurch.ca

Other Books by

Summit Global Publishing Ltd.

Living in Devotion

A 40-day devotional book by The
Summit Edmonton Church

Hope for the Broken Soul

by Louise Franck

Signs, Wonders, Miracles:

Testimonies from The Summit
Volume 1

Summit Global Publishing Ltd.

In December 2020, Tracy Belford received a vision from the Lord to open a publishing company. The purpose was to share the word of the Lord that was coming out of The Summit Edmonton Church. She was inspired by Romans 10:17 (NKJV) *"So then faith comes by hearing, and hearing by the word of God."*

Tracy believed that God was sharing so much wisdom and revelation within her church that it needed to be shared on a larger scale to increase the faith of many. To date, she has published four books:

Signs, Wonders, Miracles Volume 1

Living in Devotion: 40 Day Devotional

Month of Captivation: Prayer Journal 2023

Hope for the Broken Soul

Manufactured by Amazon.ca
Bolton, ON